What Our Readers Have Said...

"Although I consider myself a seasoned sales professional, it is helpful to have past learning's refreshed. The books were also beneficial because of the information concerning 'trends' in the sales relationship. The sales process should be viewed as dynamic since business relationships change regularly."

•

"For the particular business I am in and the type of sales calls I have, I find that the books in the Pinpoint Sales Training Series are very often applicable to how I conduct business. I would recommend them to other sales people, just not ones that are in my industry."

•

"These books provide very good concepts. It fits in well with the Bell Leadership training program that I attended in November."

•

"I use this material in these books and apply it to my customers and other employees I work with."

•

"I would like to know other topics. Is there anything on Production Management or Consultative Selling or Time Management?"

•

"These books are great tools that should be used as guidelines for our everyday

supervisory practices. You need to take the time to do a short self-evaluation when reading them."

•

"The Pinpoint Training Series delivers information that could be used in a lot different areas."

•

"I like this because I can take them with me to read at a convenient time. I feel the little time I have to spend in the office is best use on activities that directly relate to revenue opportunities. I like the short amount of time it takes to keep up with these."

•

"I prefer the self-study approach; it fits in with my schedule."

•

"My thought is that the real value of these books comes into effect when doing the action plans."

•

"Short and sweet. These books are easy to comprehend."

•

"I have enjoyed reading these books. They are relevant to today's work environment and the ongoing change in the way we manage our workforce."

•

"I do feel that these books have been very helpful to me at my job."

•

"I think a lot of the recommendations in these books are very useful, and can be applicable to everyday situations. If nothing else, it's a good reference guide to fall back upon if a situation arises in the future."

•

"These books are relevant to today's work environment and the ongoing change in the way we manage our workforce."

•

Productive Questioning Strategies

Pinpoint Sales Skill Development Training Series

TIMOTHY F. BEDNARZ

MAJORIUM
BUSINESS PRESS

Pinpoint Sales Skill Development Training Series
"Productive Questioning Strategies"
Timothy F. Bednarz

Graphic design: Monika Pawlak

Majorium Business Press
2025 Main Street
Stevens Point, WI 54481
715.342.1018 • 800.654.4935

ISBN 978-1-882181-91-9

Printed in the United States of America

Introduction

The Pinpoint Sales Skill Development Training Series is designed for targeted training and education regarding increased improvement in a specific skill or competency.

Each book within this series is designed to be easy to use, understand and apply to your job. It can be used as a basis for training individuals, as a discussion guide or as a personal training tool.

Each chapter within this book discusses a specific concept. When you have completed all eight chapters you should have a 360° perspective of the topic.

Additionally, each chapter is divided into specific sections:

- The first section provides you with an overview of the topic
- The Implications section discusses why the concept is important, and why it is important to learn and apply.
- The Strategies, Tips & Techniques to Apply section teaches how to use and apply the particular concept to your work.
- The Points to Ponder section gives you something to think about or to be discussed with a group setting. These are questions not meant to be immediately answered, but to be pondered over time.
- The Training Activity section provides you with the tools to transfer what you have learned to your job. It is designed to help create an action plan to effectively apply the concept.

Each of the topics in this series is time-tested and proven in the marketplace. They have been used by thousands of employees as training tools. Many of the users have commented that what made these books valuable, was the ability to refer to them when a problem surfaced. They indicated that they remembered reading about the exact problem. They referred back to these books and found an appropriate solution.

You will find them equally valuable as a resource in your professional development library.

Table of Contents

LEARNING OBJECTIVES:

- The value of effective questioning techniques.
- To identify the purpose and structure of questioning.
- To use questions to develop information.
- To apply effective listening to gather information.
- To effectively use questioning to advance the sale.
- To use questioning to establish commitment.

1

Effective Questioning Techniques

The most basic tool at the salesperson's disposal is the ability to utilize effective questioning skills. A skill that is often taken for granted, effective questioning is indispensable to uncovering problems, building trust and credibility, and focusing the customer on an effective solution.

Small details about customers can make a great deal of difference in the solutions a salesperson is able to offer. The problem is that many salespeople tend to interrogate rather than guide and direct an informative conversation with the use of probing questions.

IMPLICATIONS — WHAT THIS MEANS TO YOU

Information is the lifeblood of sales. Without the information to discern problems, concerns and needs, salespeople will undoubtedly face a number of stalls, objections and needless complications.

Salespeople are oftentimes reluctant to ask too many questions. They don't want to appear obtrusive and fear offending the customer, or simply feel it isn't important to gather information. However there are a number of reasons why salespeople need to possess and use good questioning skills.

Seeking pertinent information—

- Draws out facts that will ultimately lead to the solution.
- Leads to an understanding of the customer's viewpoints and feelings.

- Determines the customer's understanding of the problem.
- Develops trust, credibility and rapport with the customer.
- Uncovers hidden agendas.
- Focuses the customer toward a specific solution.

STRATEGIES, TIPS & TECHNIQUES TO APPLY

To get to the bottom of the customer's needs and concerns, salespeople must be sure to dig in the right spot. In other words, their questioning must be focused. There are a number of strategies and techniques that can be employed to improve salespeople's questioning skills, including:

Put the Customer at Ease

It is essential for the customer to understand that his or her interests take precedence. Individuals made to feel at ease and comfortable in this way are far more likely to share the information needed to produce a workable solution.

Salespeople should then begin with broad and open-ended questions. This technique to begin a conversation will work to further place the customer at ease. They should also create a logical sequence to their questions, which makes for a more natural and conversational tone.

Ask Permission

Salespeople should never assume that they have blanket permission to query a customer. It is always appropriate for them to ask whether they have permission to ask questions. This demonstrates their sensitivity and gives the customer a sense of power and control over the process, which greatly reduces their fears and anxieties.

Phrase Your Questions Carefully

Many salespeople will grill the customer rather than lead a discussion focused on the specific problem. This only puts the customer on the defensive and in a rush to terminate the interview.

The way a question is worded can either build trust or turn a conversation into an interrogation. It is essential for salespeople to guard against using words or tones that may put the customer on the defensive.

As salespeople move from question to question, they should acknowledge the customer's answers. They should avoid "that's nice" types of responses and keep their reactions genuine and interested.

Listen and Build on Responses

Salespeople should remove themselves from the conversation as quickly as possible and allow the customer to talk. They should then listen and observe the customer's responses.

As the customer answers a question, salespeople should listen for key words and phrases and craft their questions in a way that allows the customer to elaborate upon what he or she has communicated.

Use Personal Expertise

Salespeople should use their personal experience and expertise to frame and ask their questions. They should tie in their previous experiences to demonstrate their personal value as they question the customer.

Respect Time by Keeping Questions Focused and Simple

While customers are willing to give salespeople the time to develop information for their mutual benefit, today many are extremely busy.

Salespeople respect their clients' time by limiting their questioning. They use the time available to quickly reach their goals by using their questions to focus the conversation toward the purpose of the call. They should keep que ries simple and straightforward, and avoid complicated two- and three-part questions that distract the customer from the focus of the conversation.

POINTS TO PONDER – SOMETHING TO THINK ABOUT

1. How do you show your customers that you genuinely care about them as you question them? Explain.
2. How do you overcome hostility and resistance and get the customer to relax and open up to you?

TRAINING ACTIVITY – APPLICATION & ACTION PLAN

Develop a series of questions that focus the customer on their problem and the potential causes of the problem.

- The ideal way to do this is to focus on a target customer and develop your questions around him or her.
- Questions can then be adapted to meet the needs of customers in specific situations.

2

Identifying the Root of a Problem in Five Questions

Salespeople are often faced with customers who are either vague or unable to express themselves well enough to fully explain the extent of their problem or its causes. Arriving at the root of a problem can be frustrating for both the customer and the salesperson.

IMPLICATIONS — WHAT THIS MEANS TO YOU

Many service problems and their accompanying complications are a result of miscommunication. Customers either don't know why a problem exists or they are unable to clearly and concisely communicate the reasons. In many cases, the customer doesn't care and only wants the problem fixed. However, this doesn't help the salesperson, who either has to fix the problem or identify the proper resources so that they can.

It is important for salespeople to quickly identify the customer's problem. Overall customer satisfaction, loyalty and retention are all based upon the need for a quick and effective response that both solves the problem and satisfies the customer.

STRATEGIES, TIPS & TECHNIQUES TO APPLY

While salespeople are taught to use open-ended questions, there is a simple and effective method that allows them to quickly arrive at the root of any problem. This technique involves the salesperson asking the question, "Why?" five times in a specific sequence.

Every problem can be disclosed with the use of five "why" questions. When a customer voices a problem or concern, the salesperson begins by asking, "Why do you think the problem is happening?" When the customer responds, the next question will probe further by asking again, "Why do you think this is happening?" or if he or she voices a personal feeling, "Why do you feel this way?" The questioning sequence of additional "whys" continues to follow the same line of thinking. By the fifth "why" the root of the problem will be identified.

Advantages to the "five why" technique include:

Uncovers the Real Concern

Often customers only know they have a problem. Sometimes they are aware of the cause, but can only describe symptoms. With a simple problem, the solution may be equally simple, but often salespeople must quickly assess the cause so that they can use the proper resources to promptly resolve it. The "five why" technique allows salespeople to swiftly determine root causes and take the appropriate remedial actions.

Removes Emotional Responses

Most customers are frustrated with their problem and have a tendency to become emotional. The customer's emotions only further mask the symptoms and make it more difficult for salespeople to help them. The "five whys" allow salespeople to address these emotional feelings by questioning their source in a professional manner. They acknowledge the customer's frustration and provide him or her with an outlet to explain their frustrations while leading the salesperson to the root cause.

Avoids Wasting Time

When salespeople deal with a frustrated customer who is unable to clearly explain his or her problem, a great deal of time can be wasted. The longer it takes to positively respond to the customer, the more agitated and frustrated he or she becomes, and the further the problem is complicated.

Asking "five whys" allows salespeople to arrive at a prompt assessment that reduces the customer's stress and anxiety levels. When the customer's stress is reduced, he or she will become more cooperative. A positive chain of events is set into motion, making the process more effective and productive for all parties.

Produces a Positive Outcome

Asking "why" five times allows the salesperson to produce a positive outcome. This is not to say this is the only way they can do it, but by identifying root causes, the customer's problem is guaranteed to be properly resolved without the need for a callback.

POINTS TO PONDER – SOMETHING TO THINK ABOUT

1. Do you accept a customer's statements at face value or do you probe for the real causes behind their problems? Explain.
2. Do you see how this technique can save you time and frustration in identifying the real causes of problems?

TRAINING ACTIVITY – APPLICATION & ACTION PLAN

Take the time to practice the "five why" technique with an associate.

1. Identify several typical complaints or problems that your company

2. commonly experiences.
3. Practice using the "five why" technique to question and probe.
4. Use this method until you become polished and proficient at it.

3

The Value of Asking Questions

Many individuals see little value in the use and application of the right questioning techniques. For salespeople, questions are the tools of the trade. The proper use of effective questioning techniques accomplishes multiple objectives. Without them, representatives would find their tasks and assignments much more difficult to accomplish.

Effective questioning techniques include the knowledge and the application of the right types of questions in the right circumstances. Different kinds of questions have entirely different purposes and desired outcomes. They are designed to elicit the proper response at the right time. The key lies in knowing how to combine them all to produce a positive and desired outcome. Effective questioning techniques linked with a good service attitude are a powerful combination.

IMPLICATIONS — WHAT THIS MEANS TO YOU

The improper use and application of questions can produce less than favorable results. While consequences may not be disastrous, it will hinder the salesperson's ability to effectively produce consistent and positive outcomes for the customer.

First and foremost, salespeople must be able to analyze problems. Effective questions and questioning techniques are the tools that allow them to do this successfully.

STRATEGIES, TIPS & TECHNIQUES TO APPLY

The value of questioning is realized when salespeople are able to accomplish the following positive outcomes through the use and application of questions.

Show Respect

While questions have other primary objectives, one of the main reasons for the use of courteous and effective questioning is to demonstrate to the customer that he or she is both respected and valued. It clearly conveys that the company thinks he or she is important. This is a key impression that every salesperson must communicate, and the effective use of questions accomplishes this.

Gather Information

The most obvious purpose of questioning is to gather information. Effective questions allow salespeople to inquire about the problem, its history, causes, complications and other consequences. Without this essential information, salespeople are unable to adequately perform their jobs. They may be interfacing with the customer, but little else will occur until sufficient information is gathered. They will be unable to diagnose the customer's problem and understand what is needed to solve it.

Gain Insight

Effective questions allow salespeople to gain insight into a customer's problem, including the extent of it and its consequences. Many problems are not what they initially appear to be. Salespeople must be able to analyze what is happening to get insights into a possible solution. These insights should provide them with specific trigger points to include additional resources to quickly resolve the problem.

Clarify Issues

Problems will generate additional customer concerns, issues and consequences that must be also resolved. Good questions allow salespeople to probe the issues and clarify any and all concerns the customer might have. Left unresolved, many of these issues and concerns can linger and develop into bigger problems later on. Effective solutions must encompass all facets of a customer's problem. Good questioning techniques allow salespeople to identify and clarify these aspects.

Ascertain the Seriousness of the Problem

All problems are not equal. Each has its own set of consequences and repercussions. It will often depend when and where the problem occurs. Some need immediate attention, while others can take a lower priority.

Effective questions allow salespeople to ascertain the seriousness of the problem. This provides them with the means to prioritize problems and to focus the appropriate resources on their resolution. This can minimize the extent of the problem and limit the consequences to the company.

Identify the Proper Solution

The use and application of effective questioning allows salespeople to identify the proper solution, bring the right company resources into focus, and resolve the customer's problem in a quick and efficient manner.

POINTS TO PONDER — SOMETHING TO THINK ABOUT

1. In the past have you recognized the value of effective questions?
2. How much care do you take in choosing the right question during a customer contact?

TRAINING ACTIVITY — APPLICATION & ACTION PLAN

Identify a customer problem that you recently worked on or take notes on one or more situations over the next several days.

1. Recall the use of questions during each customer contact.
2. Determine if the questions you used accomplished the following objectives:
    - Show Respect
    - Gather Information
    - Gain Insight
    - Clarify Issues
    - Ascertain the Seriousness of the Problem
3. Identify the proper solution.
4. Identify the areas where you are failing to meet these objectives.
5. Formulate questions you can use in the future to fill in these voids.

4

Probing Questions That Completely Identify Problems and Needs

While salespeople will often encounter similar customer problems, it is dangerous for them to make assumptions regarding their accounts. Good questioning techniques enable salespeople to efficiently guide their customers through a polished sequence of questions that does not interrogate, but allows them to elicit information and provide a workable solution.

Effective questioning facilitates clear communication of information and solutions between the company and the customer. Many service problems stem from a poor or faulty level of communication, where the cause of the problem is not clearly comprehended and understood by the salesperson. This results in the misidentification of solutions, resulting in customer callbacks.

IMPLICATIONS — WHAT THIS MEANS TO YOU

It is important for salespeople to recognize that it does not take a properly trained individual any more time and effort to resolve a problem—even if it takes multiple calls and the involvement of other service elements within the company—than to mishandle a customer problem with poor communication and questioning techniques.

STRATEGIES, TIPS & TECHNIQUES TO APPLY

There is a series and sequence of questions that salespeople can follow to fully understand the extent and seriousness of a customer's problem. These include:

History Questions

The purpose of history questions is to gather information regarding the background, circumstances, and other pertinent facts surrounding the customer's problem. Salespeople can use these questions to verify information that they know or suspect to be the case:

- What is the problem?
- How long has it been happening?
- When did the problem start?
- How long was the product or service being used before the problem started?

Symptom Questions

Although a common service pitfall is to address symptoms instead of the core issue—resulting in a recurring problem and further callbacks—symptom questions will provide the salesperson an effective way to have the customer fully describe their problem. Symptom questions include:

- Describe exactly what is happening.
- How would you describe ____?
- What do you observe when the problem occurs?

Cause Questions

The purpose of the cause question is to determine the specific origins of the symptoms. This allows salespeople to probe more deeply into the problem and attempt to pinpoint the root cause. These questions allow salespeople to make an assessment of the problem and should trigger specific remedial actions:

- Do you have any idea what may be causing that?

- What factors bring about the problem?
- What are you doing when the problem begins?
- Does the product display any service codes or messages?

Complication Questions

Complication questions determine the seriousness of the customer's problem and the impact it is having on their job and business. These questions should indicate to the salesperson the priority the problem should take:

- How does that affect ____?
- What does the problem lead to?
- What will happen if the problem is not immediately addressed?
- What additional problems does this create for you?

Cure Questions

As not all solutions are considered equal in the customer's eyes, it is important to determine what customers perceive to be a fair solution. Cure questions allow salespeople to accomplish this. In many cases, a customer's solution is less than a company is willing to provide. Sample questions include:

- What do you want us to do?
- What would you consider an acceptable solution?
- If we did ____, would you consider that to be an acceptable solution?

Salespeople must learn to blend these questions into a smooth and polished sequence of questions that both delineates the problem and points to an acceptable solution. It is not enough to ask three or four history questions and then move on to three or four symptom questions and so on. They should develop a logical, smooth, and conversational flow to their questioning that elicits information rather than interrogating customers about their problem.

POINTS TO PONDER – SOMETHING TO THINK ABOUT

1. What approach to your customer questions have you used in the past?
2. Did your current method effectively move the customer through a logical sequence to gather information and develop solutions?

TRAINING ACTIVITY – APPLICATION & ACTION PLAN

1. Formulate three or four questions in each of the following categories:
    a. History Questions
    b. Symptom Questions
    c. Cause Questions
    d. Complication Questions
2. Select one or two questions from each category.
3. Develop a polished and effective sequence of questions that leads the customer through all categories of questions.
4. Use these questions with customers and revise the questions until you are able to handle customers in a polished and professional manner.

5

Questions That Develop Information

All questions inherently develop information. However, various questions and questioning techniques are better suited to arriving at the facts fast and in a more customer-friendly manner than others. Salespeople need to acquaint themselves with different questioning styles and how they can be used to their advantage.

Without adequate information, the salesperson cannot effectively service his or her customer's needs. In this regard, any and all types of questions and questioning techniques can be combined to achieve a successful outcome. The challenge is to become familiar with the advantages and disadvantages inherent in each type. Equipped with this knowledge, wise choices can be made to make questioning more effective and efficient.

IMPLICATIONS — WHAT THIS MEANS TO YOU

Salespeople should understand that questions should be used to clarify problems and issues in a concise and clear manner. By blending the following three types of questions, information can be productively obtained from the customer in a way that does not offend or intimidate with a steady stream of questions.

STRATEGIES, TIPS & TECHNIQUES TO APPLY

Salespeople should develop an understanding of the various types of questions in order to gather in-depth information from their customers. Each type of question has a specific role in the service process. None are inherently good or bad—all are tools that skilled sales representatives can learn to select and apply in the appropriate circumstances.

Closed-Ended Questions

Closed-ended questions are questions that allow customers to provide a limited response, typically a "yes" or "no." While these questions are restrictive in nature, there are distinct advantages and disadvantages to their use.

Advantages:

- Closed-ended questions are quick and require little time investment, just the short answer.
- Provide the salesperson with a high level of control over the customer contact.
- Can be used to obtain direct and specific answers.

Disadvantages:

- Incomplete answers require the salesperson to get more information from the customer.
- Closed-ended questions can be leading, resulting in inaccurate assumptions and conclusions.
- Discourage the customer from openly disclosing information.
- Can irritate the customer by making them feel interrogated.

Content Questions

Content questions are familiar "who" "what" "where" "when" and "how" questions. Comprising the salesperson's primary tool, these will effectively develop details and explanations of the problem with the customer.

Advantages:

- Content questions are easy and natural for salespeople to use.
- Obtain the specific facts and information related to the problem.
- Are familiar and comfortable for customers and salespeople to ask.

Disadvantages:

- Content questions may not get to the underlying issues.
- Will rarely elicit customers' true feelings and emotions.
- May cause salespeople to miss key non-technical issues and concerns.

Open-Ended Questions

Open-ended questions are those questions that allow salespeople to solicit additional information from their customers. They invite customers to talk about the problem, while establishing rapport, gathering information and increasing understanding. More importantly, they do not lead the customer.

Advantages:

- Open-ended questions develop trust.
- Are perceived less threatening by the customer.
- Allow for a greater freedom of expression.
- Probe for the issue's context.
- Measure the customer's understanding of a problem.

Disadvantages:

- Open-ended questions can be time-consuming, as customers may be long-winded in their responses.
- Can generate superfluous and irrelevant information.
- May result in the customer needing to focus his or her answers.

POINTS TO PONDER — SOMETHING TO THINK ABOUT

1. How effectively do you blend different questioning styles in your customer contacts?
2. Do you use one style of questioning more often than others?

TRAINING ACTIVITY — APPLICATION & ACTION PLAN

Develop a series of open-ended, closed-ended and content questions you can ask your customers.

1. Identify common customer scenarios and develop these three styles of questions to fit each.
2. Polish your questions and compile them in a list.
3. Refer to the list as you talk with customers.

6

Developing a Questioning Attitude

A good inquisitive nature is one of the foundations of a successful sales career. It originates in the personal attitude of the salesperson who is genuinely interested in the customer and his or her problems. A positive and caring salesperson can overcome obstacles to developing information with customers simply because he or she sincerely cares and wants to help them.

Attitude is stressed in many aspects of sales training. Salespeople are either of *service*, or of the mind their customers think they are their *servants*. In the first case, possessing the depth of discernment to understand that were they in their client's shoes they would want a solution and fast, representatives want to be *of help* to the customer. In the latter, they resentfully consider themselves ill-used servants. In both cases, the results are predictable.

IMPLICATIONS — WHAT THIS MEANS TO YOU

The salesperson's own personal attitude will determine how frequently and with what kind of effort they will choose to apply effective questioning and listening skills. It comes down to a personal choice that will impact the customer relationship and whether he or she will continue to do business with the company. Salespeople hold the power to choose an outlook of willing service. Such a choice will pay large dividends for them, their companies and their customers.

STRATEGIES, TIPS & TECHNIQUES TO APPLY

Jim Barksdale, former COO of FedEx, formed a customer service philosophy that every package should be treated as the customer's golden package—the package that could make or break their business.

Out of the millions of packages that FedEx picked up, sorted and delivered, employees were to treat every one as though it were the most important package in the world. The golden package mindset was a significant factor in FedEx becoming one of the most reliable service companies in the world.

There are many sales lessons that can be learned from this example, the most prominent of which is the attitude toward the customer. This is the pivot on which sales careers succeed or fail. Salespeople can have superior questioning and listening skills, but if they don't care about the customer and his or her problems they will be of little use.

Sales success stems from a desire to want to help the customer by fully understanding his or her problem so it can be solved as quickly as possible. This is directly based on the salesperson's personal attitude. If he or she doesn't care, they will not seek to fully investigate the problem and understand its cause. They will not care about the consequences of the problem for the company, or that with adequate customer feedback, the company may be able to address the issue internally and prevent further customer problems.

There are three cardinal rules salespeople should remember:

> **Customers don't forget attitudes.** Life is too short to deal with unpleasant people, and customers want to avoid conflict. People involved in a chain of events with a salesperson who has a sour attitude and doesn't care about serving the customer will not soon forget—but *will* pursue other alternatives for the product or service they need.
>
> **Customers don't forget how issues and misunderstandings were handled.** More than any other time in a customer's relationship with a company, when problems, issues and misunderstandings occur, there is no better opportunity to strengthen the relationship. This is why good questioning and listening skills are critical. They convey that the salesperson cares and that the customer is important and valued.

Customers don't forget how they are handled after the sale. Customers measure a company's value and performance by their total experience: the purchase, the product's application, and the service they receive thereafter. However, when problems occur and accounts are not treated with respect and their issue is not addressed quickly, this is what is remembered and this is what the company is evaluated upon.

Good questioning and listening techniques linked with a positive and pleasant service attitude assure customer satisfaction. It is a critical element in the total service package provided by salespeople.

POINTS TO PONDER — SOMETHING TO THINK ABOUT

1. Are you more caring and concerned about the customer on some days than others?
2. Do you feel your personal attitude affects your job, the customers you serve and the best interests of your company?

TRAINING ACTIVITY — APPLICATION & ACTION PLAN

1. Think of three examples where your personal attitude determined how well you questioned and cared about the customer's problems.
2. Analyze each example and determine the possible impact it had on you, the customer and the company.

7

How Well Do You Listen?

Effective listening and questioning skills are closely linked. Questioning becomes worthless without the ability to clearly hear and precisely interpret what customers have to say.

There are multiple levels of listening that salespeople must be attuned to. Each ultimately affects how they respond to their customers, and how customer relationships are impacted.

IMPLICATIONS – WHAT THIS MEANS TO YOU

Listening is emphasized as a critical service skill for all salespeople to master but goes well beyond passively absorbing what customers are saying. It involves focusing directly on what is being said and implied, reading between the lines, analyzing what is being communicated and determining how to craft sales approaches that meet individual customer needs.

This means responding to what customers are saying with well thought-out responses. Many salespeople tend to ignore or brush aside customer comments, thoughts and concerns, and—rather than registering and acknowledging them—instead say what they want to say. This creates a complete disconnect, with little or no real communication going on between salespeople and their customers.

It is important for salespeople to pose specific questions to customers, and then get out of the way of their answers. They should be allowed to speak without interruption in order to provide vital information. Salespeople need to make it a point to interject with more probing questions so as to arrive at the heart of an unclear or possibly misinterpreted issue or thought.

STRATEGIES, TIPS & TECHNIQUES TO APPLY

While salespeople enjoy talking about themselves, their jobs, families and a host of other subjects they feel are important—including even product specifications—telling is not helping. Real two-way communication takes place when both parties discuss issues and applicable solutions of mutual importance.

With this in mind, there are five levels of listening salespeople should be aware of. Three of them completely undermine their professional stance as a good listener, while the other two can greatly improve the customer inquiry and discussion process. Each affects the outcome of conversations and dialogues and impacts the customer relationship building process. These levels are:

Preoccupied

At this level, salespeople are distracted from listening. They tend to concentrate on their notes or on gathering information to impart to their customers, or they may simply allow their minds to wander onto other things. They are preoccupied with something other than listening to what their customers are saying and questioning and thus lose valuable information and input. This leaves customers with a strong impression that what they have to say is not important, which translates into the belief that their business is not valued either.

Feigned

Pretending to hear what customers are saying is the most common level of listening salespeople attain. They look attentive and make the appropriate motions to show they are listening, but in reality they are preparing to speak.

The most common consequence of feigned listening is a loss of credibility in the eyes of customers. This is because salespeople often respond with either totally unrelated or unemotional statements. It demonstrates a lack of respect for their customers and undermines the ability to build an atmosphere of trust. The levels of true care and concern with these types of salespeople are transparently shallow, which often leaves customers feeling insulted and undervalued.

Selective

While salespeople are listening, they sometimes allow their biases and preconceived notions to filter and distort what is being said. They determine what is relevant, which then limits what they can learn. Selective listening often creates faulty perceptions of customer-related needs. This can lead to poorly crafted solutions or situations where salespeople are blindsided by their customers' reactions and responses.

Attentive

Attentive listening is active listening. Salespeople are able to demonstrate their listening skills and ability to hear by paraphrasing and actively acknowledging what is said with responses that accurately reflect their customers' comments, internal feelings and concerns. However, at this level, many salespeople are not emotionally engaged. The appearance of emotional connection may be created, but salespeople at this level are not totally connected to their customers.

Empathetic

At this level, salespeople are emotionally invested in each contact. They are able to "think outside of the box" and view situations from their customers' viewpoints. They are genuinely concerned about their problems, issues, thoughts, feelings, suggestions, and frustrations. When customers know their representatives care about them and will do everything possible to ensure their concerns are fully heard and addressed, they are then much more inclined to hear about what they have to offer.

Salespeople genuinely interested in developing a customer focus must learn how to hear and accurately interpret the intents, implications and feelings behind what is being conveyed to them. The impression they want to create is one of an external focus aimed directly at their customers' satisfaction and importance.

POINTS TO PONDER — SOMETHING TO THINK ABOUT

1. While salespeople fall into every listening level mentioned above at one time or another, what level do you normally achieve during average customer contacts? Explain.
2. What do you need to do to elevate your listening skills to the next level or better?

TRAINING ACTIVITY — APPLICATION & ACTION PLAN

1. Identify sales encounters that reflect every level of listening mentioned above.
2. Explain the situation, the circumstances and results.
3. Compare several of your contacts and derive a lesson from your experiences.

8

Effective Questioning

It is often thought that effective questioning is the result of good intuition rather than outwardly applying a skillful approach. This may have been true of years past, but with today's customers it becomes essential to be able to solve problems that are more complex than ever before. Along with the increasing complexity of problems, salespeople must also deal daily with heightened and more demanding than ever customer expectations. To satisfy them, it is imperative to use effective questioning skills and approaches. It only takes one mistake to leave a situation unresolved or a solution less than desirable, and the company can lose a significant source of revenue.

Sales success requires setting individual goals for effective questioning, and applying the most beneficial methods to get customers to open up and completely disclose situations, feelings, reasoning, and expectations. Good questioning takes careful planning, with key outcomes defined, significant sequences determined, and activities to advance the solution all structured and directly connected to the questioning and communication process.

IMPLICATIONS — WHAT THIS MEANS TO YOU

The questioning and communication planning process must be used as a guide to bring about the best possible outcome or solution. The key is to produce a highly productive atmosphere to meet customer expectations and generate ideas that translate into effective problem solving.

Questioning, interaction and imagination are the three major elements that bring it all together. Planning and utilizing the right techniques allows customers and salespeople to communicate across barriers that otherwise work to hinder the process.

STRATEGIES, TIPS & TECHNIQUES TO APPLY

There are seven planned techniques that work well to eliminate barriers to meeting customer expectations and solving their problems in a timely and courteous manner.

Know Something About the Customer

Salespeople should learn as much as they can up front about the customer, and plan to begin their questioning process by trying to get a sense of both their expectations and the rules they play by. They should determine the boundaries that define the problem or situation and stay within them. This works much better for eliminating problems that surface and must be addressed before the encounter ends.

Use Appropriate Terms

Salespeople should guard against using slang, work jargon or idioms that can muddy or garble their message or the area in which they are questioning the customer. Professional questions are formulated to be clear, short and to the point. They must be focused in order to elicit the exact information needed. The use of inappropriate terms is indicative of a lack of professionalism, and serves only to confuse customers and lengthen the problem solving process.

Use a Softer Tone

Salespeople should make a point of softening their voice when talking to their customers. It is common to talk louder, especially when one is having trouble understanding something over the phone or when emotions have come to the fore of the questioning and communication process. Yet a raised voice can easily convey the wrong message. Some clients will resent being treated as though they are hearing impaired when they are only trying to carefully comprehend certain questions and comments. Others will believe the salesperson is talking down to them rather than simply attempting to be of service.

Speak Calmly, Slowly and Clearly

As customers are prone to lose interest when the salesperson speaks too rapidly, the most pivotal questions should be communicated in a calm, clear and concise manner, with a slower than normal speed. When customers are exposed to fast-paced questioning and abrupt shifts in subjects, barriers are created, and meanings and interpretations are often obscured and sometimes lost. A professional salesperson gives customers every chance to register every word, phrase and implication and to derive direct meaning from the sequential questions being asked.

Repeat

If a customer asks to have a question repeated for clarity of understanding, it is important for salespeople not to add to or omit any of the words used initially. Rather, they should repeat exactly what they said with the same inflections and tone. They should not say, "let me put it another way"—the customer's mind is already focused on the words they just heard, and they only want to clarify some of those they missed. When, upon repeating, the whole question is altered, its intent and meaning is lost in translation. This only adds confusion to the questioning process.

Encourage Questions

As part of the problem solving process, salespeople need to be open and do everything in their power to encourage their customers to ask questions. They should remember that some customers are reluctant to admit to confusion or ignorance on subjects. Encouraging clients to ask questions requires two deliberate actions: urging them to openly ask questions anytime they wish, and making certain to treat them with respect and dignity when they do. Otherwise, most of these shy customers may never ask for help or support again, and will often even decide to take their business elsewhere.

Facilitate and Reinforce Communication and Questioning

Salespeople should carefully plan the endings to their questioning and inquiry process and all subsequent conversations. It is vital to remember that a customer encounter should never end abruptly once issues are completely addressed. Instead, the skillful approach is to take the time to summarize the important points covered within the total questioning process and resultant discussions. Summarizing critical points, issues, facts and data slowly and clearly is essential to preventing misinterpretations of communicated messages. This is a highly effective "safety net" action, as going over what was said, addressed and developed will not only help to prevent misunderstandings, but will also actively demonstrate personal friendliness and customer importance.

POINTS TO PONDER — SOMETHING TO THINK ABOUT

1. Do you do everything you can to encourage your customers to ask questions in regard to issues and concerns during the questioning process?
2. Do you make it a point to repeat important information or questions in order to make them clearly understood?

TRAINING ACTIVITY — APPLICATION & ACTION PLAN

1. Identify a specific customer.
2. Analyze the questioning encounter to see if all the following elements were incorporated.
    - Know Something About the Customer
    - Use Appropriate Terms
    - Use a Softer Voice

- Speak Calmly, Slowly and Clearly
- Repeat Critical Facts, Data and Questions
- Encourage Questions
- Facilitate and Reinforce Communication and Questioning

About the Author

Timothy F. Bednarz, Ph.D. is CEO of the American Management Development Group, Inc. For over 20 years he has researched, designed and authored hundreds of learning and development programs used by Fortune 1000 companies.

He is also the author of *Great! What Makes Leaders Great. What They Did, How They Did It and What You Can Learn from It* (2011).

Speaking Availability

Timothy F. Bednarz, Ph.D. is available for speaking engagements for your next meeting or association event. He can be contacted at 800-654-4935 or by e-mail at timothy.bednarz@majorium.com.

Bulk Sales

Bulk sales of this book or any other titles available from Majorium Business Press. Inquiries can be directed to sales@majorium.com, or by phone at 800-6654-4935.

Quick Order Form

Fax orders: 715-342-1118. Send this form.

Telephone orders: Call 800-654-4935 toll-free. Have your credit card ready.

Email orders: sales@majorium.com

Postal orders: Majorium Business Press, 2025 Main Street, Stevens Point, WI 54481, USA.

Please send the following books:

____

____

____

____

Please send more FREE information on:

❑Catalog ❑Speaking/Seminars ❑Mailing Lists ❑Consulting

Name: ____

Address: ____

City: ______________________ State: ____ Zip: ________

Telephone: ______________________________________

Email address: ___________________________________

Sales tax: Please add 5.5% for products shipped to Wisconsin addresses.

Shipping by air:

United States: $4.00 for first book and $2.00 for each additional product.

International: $9.00 for first book; $5.00 for each additional product (estimate).

Made in United States
Cleveland, OH
06 November 2026

47678351R10026